KU-572-118

Withdrawn from Stock
Dublin City Public Libraries

Leabharlanna Poibli Chathair Bhaile Átha Cliath
Dublin City Public Libraries

Flowchart
Science

The
BRAIN

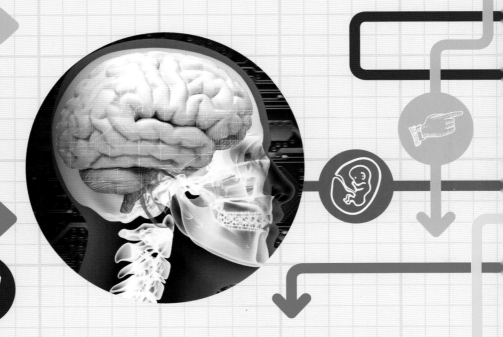

Richard and Louise Spilsbury

raintree
a Capstone company — publishers for children

Raintree is an imprint of Capstone Global Library Limited, a company incorporated in England and Wales
having its registered office at 264 Banbury Road, Oxford, OX2 7DY – Registered company number: 6695582

www.raintree.co.uk
myorders@raintree.co.uk

Text © Capstone Global Library Limited 2018
The moral rights of the proprietor have been asserted.

All rights reserved. No part of this publication may be reproduced in any form or by any means (including
photocopying or storing it in any medium by electronic means and whether or not transiently or incidentally
to some other use of this publication) without the written permission of the copyright owner, except in
accordance with the provisions of the Copyright, Designs and Patents Act 1988 or under the terms of a
licence issued by the Copyright Licensing Agency, Saffron House, 6–10 Kirby Street, London EC1N 8TS
(www.cla.co.uk). Applications for the copyright owner's written permission should be addressed to
the publisher.

Produced for Raintree by Calcium
Editors: Sarah Eason and Harriet McGregor
Designers: Paul Myerscough and Simon Borrough
Picture researcher: Rachel Blount
Originated by Capstone Global Library Limited © 2018
Printed and bound in India

ISBN 978 1 4747 6579 4
22 21 20 19 18
10 9 8 7 6 5 4 3 2 1

British Library Cataloguing in Publication Data
A full catalogue record for this book is available from the British Library.

Acknowledgements
Cover art: Shutterstock: Denk Creatives
Picture credits: Shutterstock: Blamb 37t, Jaromir Chalabala 30–31, Hung Chung Chih 14–15, Chombosan
17, CLIPAREA I Custom media 15t, Creativa Images 34, Djem 44, Juergen Faelchle 28, Sergey Furtaev 24,
Robert J. Gatto 13, Gorillaimages 41, Jiang Dao Hua 8–9, Natee K Jindakum 23r, Sebastian Kaulitzki 18,
Kzenon 40, Mhatzapa 33, 38, Nata-Lia 20–21, NPaveIN 21t, Sura Nualpradid 35, Nulinukas 11, Anna Om
22–23, Oneinchpunch 26bl, Claudia Paulussen 4–5, Posteriori 1, 6–7, Postolit 36, Pressmaster 4b, Reenya
42, 43, Rido 44–45, S-ts 19, Sciencepics 9c, Tropical studio 26–27, Vitstudio 7r, Wavebreakmedia 12b, 29.

Every effort has been made to contact copyright holders of material reproduced in this book. Any omissions
will be rectified in subsequent printings if notice is given to the publisher.

All the internet addresses (URLs) given in this book were valid at the time of going to press. However, due
to the dynamic nature of the internet, some addresses may have changed, or sites may have changed or
ceased to exist since publication. While the author and publisher regret any inconvenience this may cause
readers, no responsibility for any such changes can be accepted by either the author or the publisher.

Contents

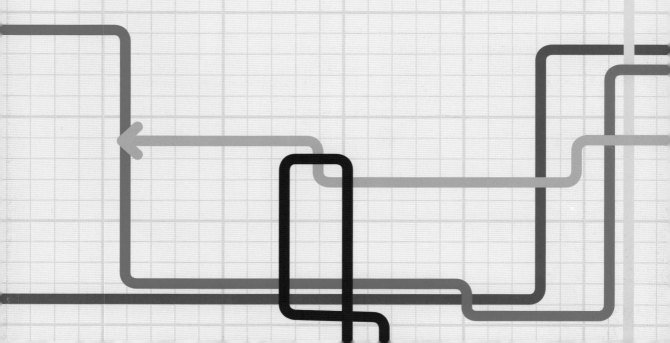

Chapter 1
The amazing brain

The human brain is incredible. It is the control centre of the whole human body. It processes huge amounts of information from all over the body. Scientists have discovered that the human brain makes about a billion billion calculations every second.

The brain controls and works with the nervous system. The **nervous system** is the network of **nerves** that carry information between the brain and the rest of the body. Nerves collect information about the world around us: the things we see, hear, feel, smell and taste. They send that information to the brain so it can work out how to respond to the different **stimuli**.

The human brain processes more information and does more calculations in 1 second than a supercomputer.

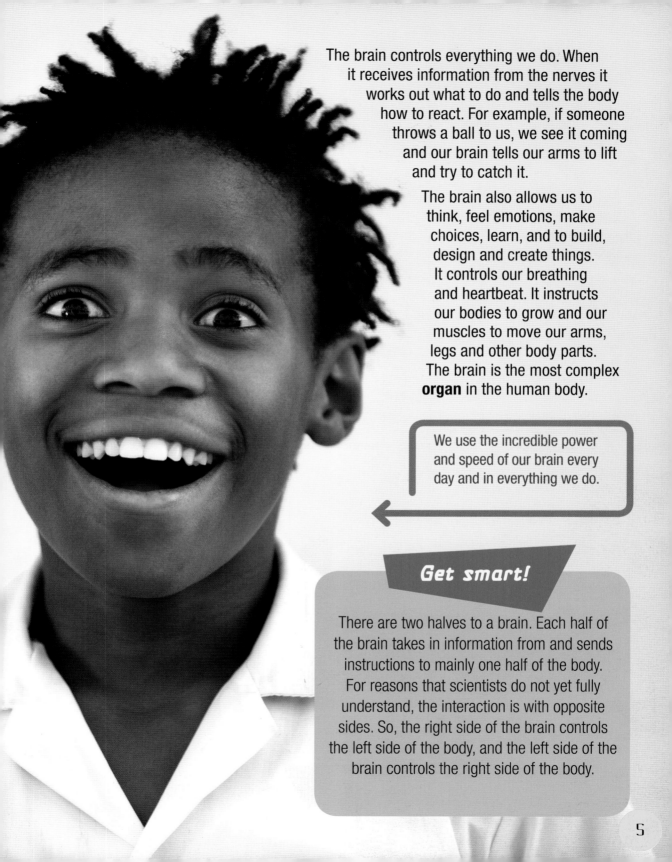

The brain controls everything we do. When it receives information from the nerves it works out what to do and tells the body how to react. For example, if someone throws a ball to us, we see it coming and our brain tells our arms to lift and try to catch it.

The brain also allows us to think, feel emotions, make choices, learn, and to build, design and create things. It controls our breathing and heartbeat. It instructs our bodies to grow and our muscles to move our arms, legs and other body parts. The brain is the most complex **organ** in the human body.

We use the incredible power and speed of our brain every day and in everything we do.

Get smart!

There are two halves to a brain. Each half of the brain takes in information from and sends instructions to mainly one half of the body. For reasons that scientists do not yet fully understand, the interaction is with opposite sides. So, the right side of the brain controls the left side of the body, and the left side of the brain controls the right side of the body.

The brain up close

The brain is one of the body's biggest organs. Inside an adult's head, this mass of pink, wrinkly, sponge-like material weighs almost 1.4 kilograms (3 pounds). The brain is roughly spherical in shape and has grooves and folds across its surface.

The brain consists of approximately 100 billion **neurons** (nerve cells), and **tissue** that support the neurons. There are also a lot of glial cells, which support and protect the neurons. The brain tissue is composed of about 75 per cent water and a lot of fat. If you stretched the brain's **blood vessels** out in one line, they would measure about 161,000 kilometres (100,000 miles), end to end.

The skull protects the brain. This hard case consists of 22 bones joined together. Three thin but tough **membranes** called meninges also cover the brain. The spaces between the meninges are filled with cerebrospinal fluid. This is a watery substance produced by cells in hollow spaces in the brain, called ventricles. The fluid flows through the ventricles and into the spaces between the meninges. It forms a cushion for the brain to stop it hitting against the inside of the skull.

The human brain is so important and delicate that it needs a lot of protection. The skull is about 1.2 cm (0.5 inches) thick in places.

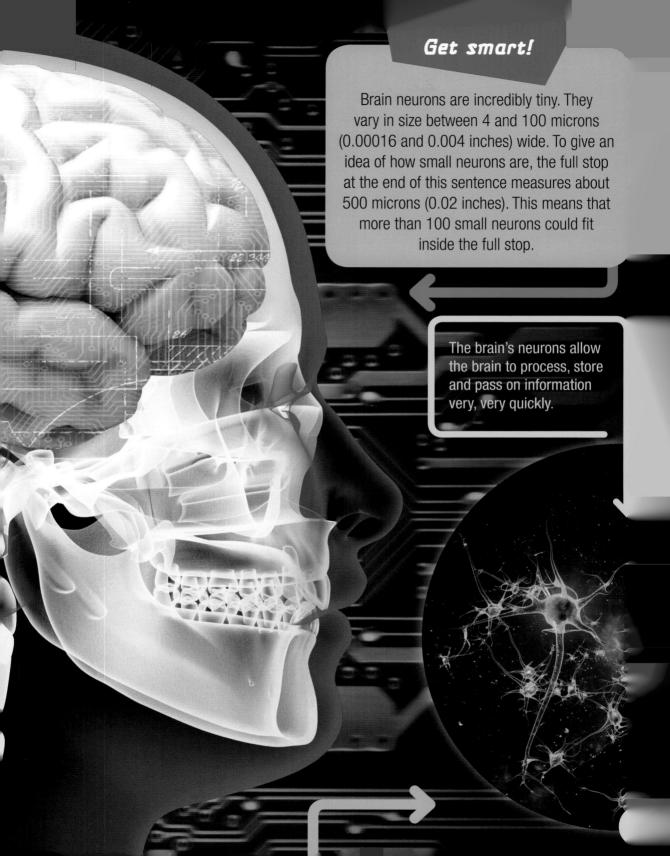

Brain neurons are incredibly tiny. They vary in size between 4 and 100 microns (0.00016 and 0.004 inches) wide. To give an idea of how small neurons are, the full stop at the end of this sentence measures about 500 microns (0.02 inches). This means that more than 100 small neurons could fit inside the full stop.

The brain's neurons allow the brain to process, store and pass on information very, very quickly.

The brain has different parts that control different activities. The largest part is the **cerebrum** and it forms the upper part of the brain. The cerebrum uses information from the senses to tell us what is going on around us and how our body should respond.

The cerebrum has two halves, called the left and right cerebral hemispheres. Each half is made up of four parts called lobes. The frontal lobes are used for speech, thought, learning, feeling emotions and movement. The parietal lobes behind them process information from the senses such as touch, temperature and pain. At the back of the brain the occipital lobes process sight. The temporal lobes, near the temples (sides of the head), are involved with hearing and memory.

The **cerebellum** is at the back of the brain beneath the cerebrum. It controls balance and complex actions such as walking and running. It helps make movements smooth and controlled and stops you falling over when you turn around.

The **brain stem** is at the base of the brain. It connects the brain to the **spinal cord** and controls some of the most basic and most important body functions. It keeps the heart beating, keeps us breathing and controls body temperature. It also helps regulate sleep and wake cycles.

The **hypothalamus** is a small but important part of the brain. It produces many **hormones**, which are chemical substances that help control different cells and organs. These hormones control functions such as thirst, hunger, sleep and mood.

The cerebellum helps this gymnast keep her balance, stand on her hands and move in a coordinated way. Without the cerebellum she would fall off.

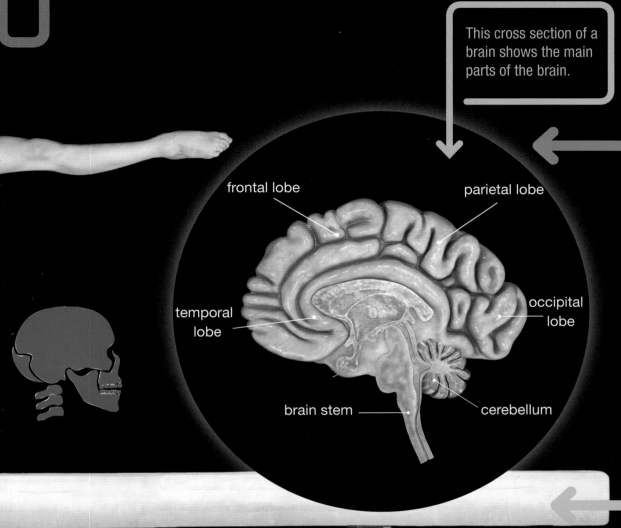

This cross section of a brain shows the main parts of the brain.

frontal lobe

parietal lobe

temporal lobe

occipital lobe

brain stem

cerebellum

Get smart!

Some animals, such as elephants, dolphins and whales, have larger brains than humans, yet they are not as intelligent. That is because although our overall brain is smaller, humans have the most developed cerebrum.

Get flow chart smart!

Brain protection

Follow the steps in this flow chart to see how your brain is protected from bumps.

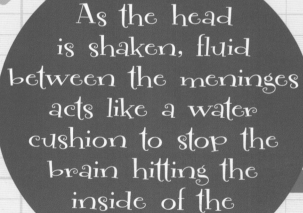

A person accidentally walks into a door and hits his head.

As the head is shaken, fluid between the meninges acts like a water cushion to stop the brain hitting the inside of the hard skull.

Flowchart Smart

Chapter 2
The brain at work

The brain uses a lot of **energy**. In fact, it uses up to one-fifth of all the energy your body receives from food. The brain uses a lot of energy because it has so many different jobs to do.

Scientists believe that two-thirds of the energy that the brain uses is spent helping neurons send signals. The other third is used for keeping the **cells** healthy. When the brain is active – for example when you do your homework – only one-third of the energy is used for cell maintenance. When the brain is inactive – such as when you sleep – more of the energy is used for maintaining the brain cells.

The food we eat is broken down by the **digestive system** and sent around the body in the blood.

Like the rest of the body, the brain functions best at a temperature of 37° C (98.6° F). In the body, the brain's **hypothalamus** controls our core temperature. It triggers changes that alter body temperature. For example, if the body is too hot, the brain tells the sweat glands to release sweat. As the sweat evaporates (turns into water vapour) from the skin, the body loses heat. If the body is too cold, the brain tells muscles to shiver. This creates heat, which warms the core body temperature.

Exercise makes you hot. The hypothalamus responds to this rise in temperature by telling your sweat glands to produce sweat.

Get smart!

Brain scans show increased blood flow when the brain is at work, which proves that thinking uses a lot of energy. The problem is that the brain cannot store much energy. That may be why complex tasks can sometimes make your brain feel tired out.

Busy all the time

The brain works non-stop, using energy even when we are asleep.

We control many of the things that our brain and nervous system do. For example, if we decide to pick up a book, our hands move towards the bookshelf because we have made the decision that they should. This type of action is described as voluntary. Many of the signals carried by nerves to and from the brain, however, are not voluntary. They happen without us thinking about, or even being aware of, them. For example, our body processes take place all the time, without us thinking about them. The signals that cause these processes to take place happen automatically.

During sleep in children and adolescents, the pituitary gland in the brain produces growth hormone. This causes the body to grow.

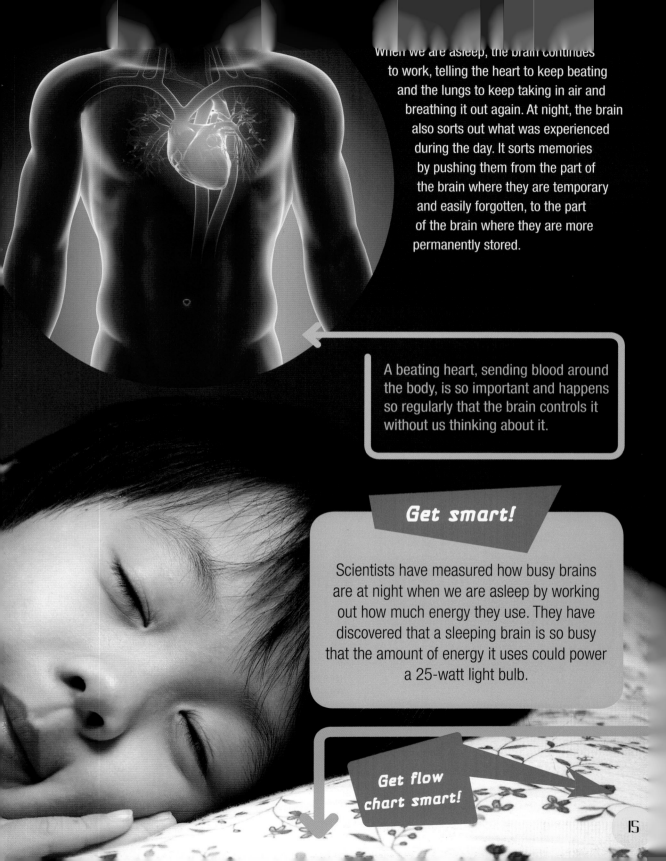

When we are asleep, the brain continues to work, telling the heart to keep beating and the lungs to keep taking in air and breathing it out again. At night, the brain also sorts out what was experienced during the day. It sorts memories by pushing them from the part of the brain where they are temporary and easily forgotten, to the part of the brain where they are more permanently stored.

A beating heart, sending blood around the body, is so important and happens so regularly that the brain controls it without us thinking about it.

Get smart!

Scientists have measured how busy brains are at night when we are asleep by working out how much energy they use. They have discovered that a sleeping brain is so busy that the amount of energy it uses could power a 25-watt light bulb.

Get flow chart smart!

Brain and body temperature

This flow chart shows how the brain keeps the body at a healthy temperature.

A person is out for a midday walk in the sun.

Her skin senses that the temperature is hot and making her body too hot.

The sweat glands produce sweat, which helps cool her down as sweat evaporates from her skin.

Nerves carry messages from the skin to the brain to warn about this increase in temperature.

The signal is directed to the hypothalamus.

The hypothalamus sends signals to the sweat glands.

Flowchart

Smart

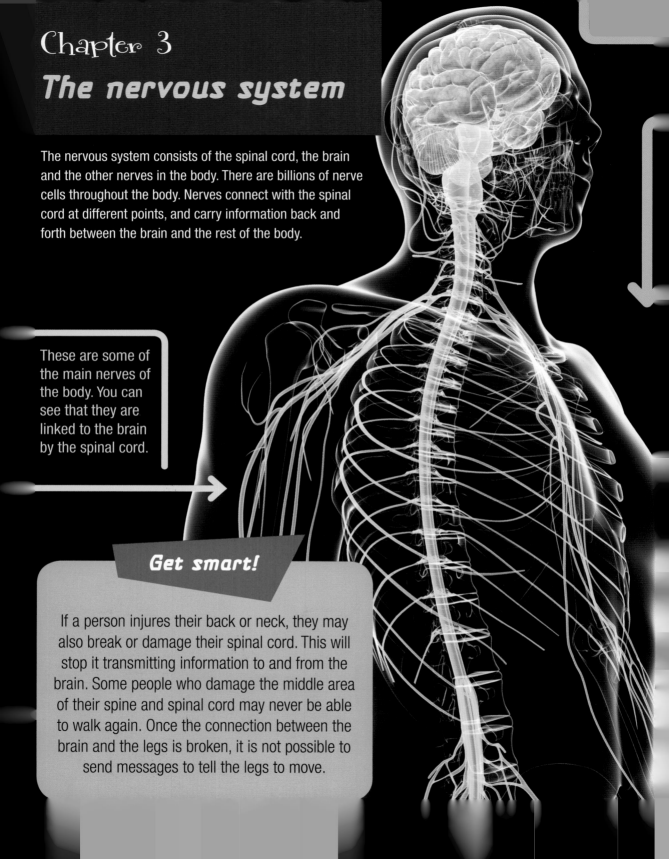

Chapter 3
The nervous system

The nervous system consists of the spinal cord, the brain and the other nerves in the body. There are billions of nerve cells throughout the body. Nerves connect with the spinal cord at different points, and carry information back and forth between the brain and the rest of the body.

These are some of the main nerves of the body. You can see that they are linked to the brain by the spinal cord.

Get smart!

If a person injures their back or neck, they may also break or damage their spinal cord. This will stop it transmitting information to and from the brain. Some people who damage the middle area of their spine and spinal cord may never be able to walk again. Once the connection between the brain and the legs is broken, it is not possible to send messages to tell the legs to move.

The spinal cord is a bundle of nerves inside, and protected by, the bones of the spine (backbone). It is about 2 centimetres (1 inch) thick and up to 40 cm (16 inches) long in adults. The nerves of the spinal cord carry information between the brain and the outer nerves of the body. Other nerves go directly from the brain to the eyes, ears and other parts of the head. The spinal cord and brain together make up the central nervous system.

Nerve signals or messages are called **impulses**. Impulses begin in **receptors**. For example, when your fingers touch a rough surface, receptors in the skin sense the change and create an impulse. The impulse travels through nerves to the part of the brain that can recognize the information. It works out what you are touching. If you need to move your fingers off the surface, the brain sends impulses to tell the muscles to move the fingers.

Neurons can relay messages at speeds of more than 300 kph (190 mph) to respond quickly to a change.

How nerves work

Nerves consist of bundles of long, thin neurons (nerve cells), connected together like links in a chain. The neurons are perfectly structured to pass information extremely quickly.

The neurons that carry messages between the brain and the rest of the body have branching ends called **dendrites**. The long, thread-like parts that connect them and along which impulses are carried are called **axons**. An impulse travels in one direction, through the cell body of the neuron and along the axon. An impulse is like a short burst of electricity and flows from neuron to neuron, to and from the brain and different parts of the body.

Impulses travel from neuron to neuron faster than a sprinting athlete. The place where a signal passes from one neuron to another is called a **synapse**. This is a small gap between the two neurons. To pass the impulse along, the axon releases chemicals called neurotransmitters across the synapse.

There is a layer of insulation around the axons of nerve cells to stop signals escaping, a little like there is a layer of insulating plastic around an electrical wire.

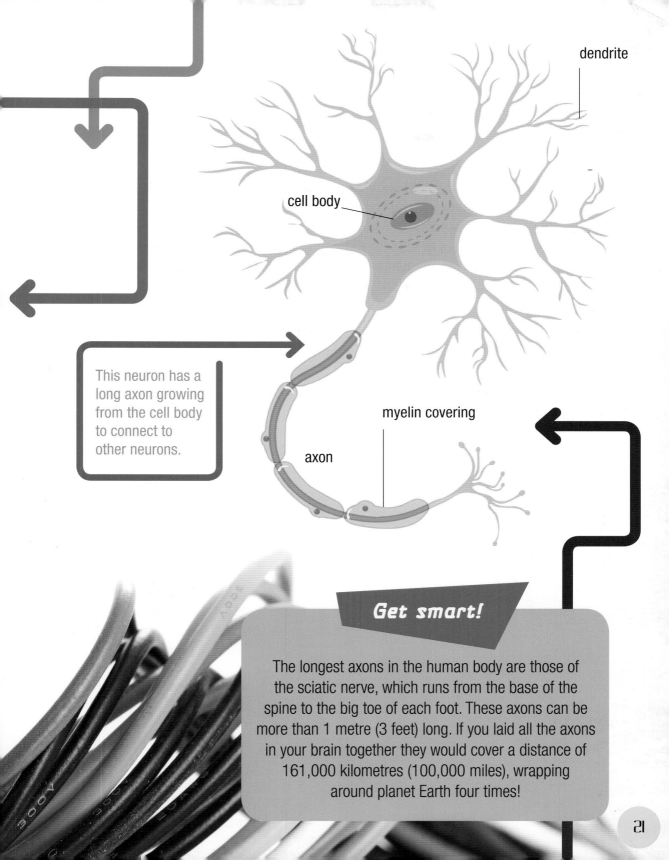

dendrite

cell body

This neuron has a
long axon growing
from the cell body
to connect to
other neurons.

myelin covering

axon

Get smart!

The longest axons in the human body are those of
the sciatic nerve, which runs from the base of the
spine to the big toe of each foot. These axons can be
more than 1 metre (3 feet) long. If you laid all the axons
in your brain together they would cover a distance of
161,000 kilometres (100,000 miles), wrapping
around planet Earth four times!

The senses

The information that the brain receives about the world around us is gathered by our senses. Our senses of touch, sight, hearing, smell and taste detect information using special cells or nerve endings.

Most of our senses rely on sense organs. Sense organs include the eyes, skin and ears. Sense organs contain receptors. The receptors respond to changes. For example, the retina at the back of the eye responds to changing patterns of light. It sends impulses along a large nerve to the brain so that we can see. Receptors in the ear detect sound waves (vibrations) in the air. The sound receptors create nerve impulses that they send to the brain to interpret.

Receptors are groups of cells that detect changes in the environment such as different smells, colours and textures.

The nose has more than 10 million smell receptors that send patterns of impulses to the brain so it can identify different smells. We get our sense of taste from receptors called taste buds in the mouth.

The skin is a very special sense organ. To give us a sense of touch, there are touch receptors in the skin that covers our whole body. These receptors are made up of nerve endings. The nerve endings sense changes in things such as **pressure** and temperature. Some nerve endings can sense when an object feels hot or cold and others can sense a gentle touch.

Walking in soft, dry sand can feel good because the toes and feet are among the most sensitive parts of the body.

Get smart!

Some areas of the body's skin are more sensitive than others. The fingertips, lips and toes are all very sensitive because they have more receptor cells in them than other, less sensitive areas.

Get flow
chart smart!

Nerves

Follow this flow chart to find out how nerves work.

Touch receptors in the skin sense a change in pressure.

They transmit signals to neurons to carry the message to the brain.

In this way, the signal travels very quickly all the way to the brain.

Impulses travel from the longest axon of one neuron to the shortest dendrite on the next.

At the gap between neurons (the synapse), the axon releases chemicals called neurotransmitters.

The neurotransmitters carry signals across the narrow gap that separates one neuron from another.

Flowchart

Smart

Chapter 4
Reflexes

When a receptor is stimulated it usually sends a signal to the central nervous system and the brain controls the response. If a very quick response is needed, however, a reflex action happens. This does not involve the brain at all.

Reflex actions happen when you touch something very hot or sharp. The body must pull the hand away very quickly to avoid injury. You do not have to think about moving your hand. It happens automatically. In a reflex action, instead of nerve signals going to the brain, they go to the spinal cord and out again. Reactions that involve the brain are quick, but bypassing the brain in times of danger makes the action immediate.

One common simple reflex action happens when we step outside on a sunny day. The eyes warn the brain that the light is too bright. The brain quickly tells muscles in the eyes to make the pupils smaller. The pupils are the tiny black holes in the centre of the iris, the coloured part of the eye. If too much light enters the eyes through the pupil, it could damage them. The brain automatically shrinks the pupils to ensure this does not happen.

The way the eyes and brain react to bright light to make pupils smaller is called the light reflex.

A baby's reflex actions include grasping and sucking. This means they can grab on to things if they need to, and drink the milk they need to survive their first weeks of life. Babies also have a reflex action that makes a flap in their throat close if they suddenly go under water. This dive reflex means that babies automatically hold their breath and open their eyes when under water.

Babies also have a swim reflex. If supported tummy-side down in water, they move their arms and legs in a swimming motion.

How reflexes work

Reflex reactions happen fast so the body can protect itself. By sending signals in a loop to the spinal cord and back, reflex actions can be instantaneous.

A simple nerve circuit called a reflex arc controls reflex actions. Sensory neurons respond to signals from the senses. They send signals to the spinal cord through relay neurons. Special neurons in the spinal cord connect directly with motor neurons. Motor neurons send signals to the muscles. They operate the part of the body that must move quickly.

Reflex actions happen to allow an immediate response if we touch something very hot.

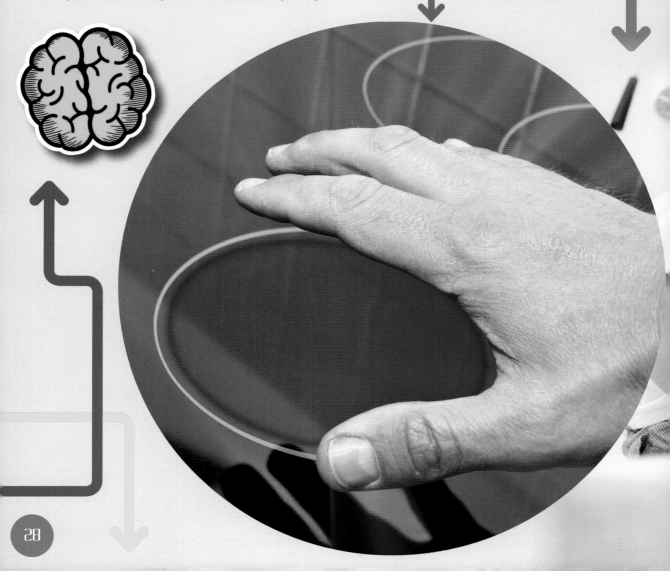

Reflexes are so important that doctors carry out tests to be sure they are working properly. They usually do the knee-jerk test. First, the patient sits with knees bent and one leg crossed over the other so that the upper foot hangs clear of the floor. The doctor gives a quick, sharp tap just below the kneecap with a small hammer. This sends signals to the spinal cord to instruct the leg muscles to react with a reflex action and the leg instantly kicks up. If this happens, the doctor knows that the nervous system is working properly. This reflex is designed to help you keep your balance if your leg is knocked.

Get smart!

As a reflex action happens, signals also pass a message to the brain. That is why you feel the pain almost at the same time, or sometimes just after, you move your hand away from something hot or sharp.

It takes some people a few taps for sense receptors to respond to the knee-jerk test.

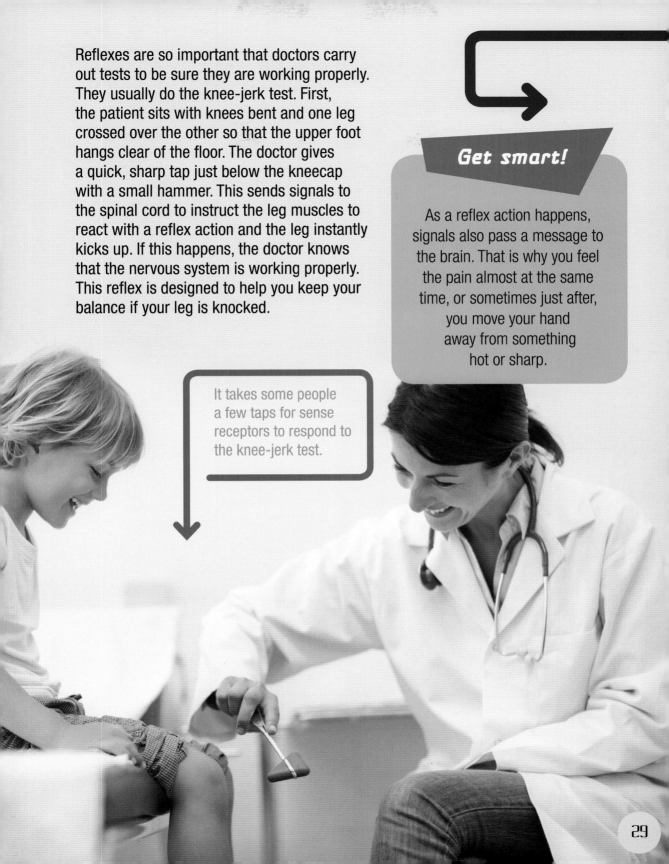

On automatic

Some reflex actions are with us from the moment we are born. These are in-built, **innate** behaviours. The body also develops some reflex actions as we grow older. These reactions are known as conditioned reflexes, and they do involve the brain.

Get smart!

A Russian scientist called Ivan Pavlov carried out a series of experiments to demonstrate a conditioned reflex. Every time he fed his dog, he rang a bell. After a while, the dog began to salivate at the sound of the bell, even when no food was present. The ringing of the bell became a conditioned stimulus.

Have you ever wondered why your mouth fills with saliva when you smell your favourite food cooking? This is an example of a conditioned reflex. The brain recognizes the smell based on previous experiences of eating that food. It automatically creates the reflex response that makes salivation occur. The reason for producing saliva is to get the body ready to digest food.

People can sometimes stop some innate and conditioned reflex actions if they really think about it. If someone decides to keep their hand on something that is really too hot to hold or keep a finger on something sharp, they can. That is because the strength of the nerve impulses from the brain is stronger than those from the reflex arc. While it is usually not a good idea to do this, it does enable us, for example, to hold on to a hot dinner plate when otherwise we might drop it.

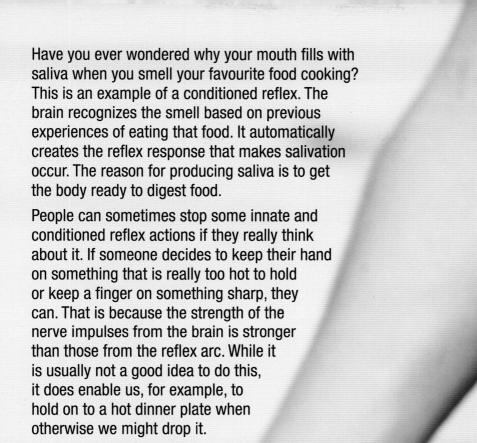

As soon as a dog smells food, it will begin to salivate in preparation for eating the food.

Get flow chart smart!

Reflex actions

This flow chart follows the steps that occur in a reflex action.

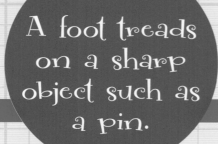

A foot treads on a sharp object such as a pin.

Messages from the motor neurons tell the muscles in the leg to move the foot away quickly.

Neurons that connect to the brain make the person aware of the pain.

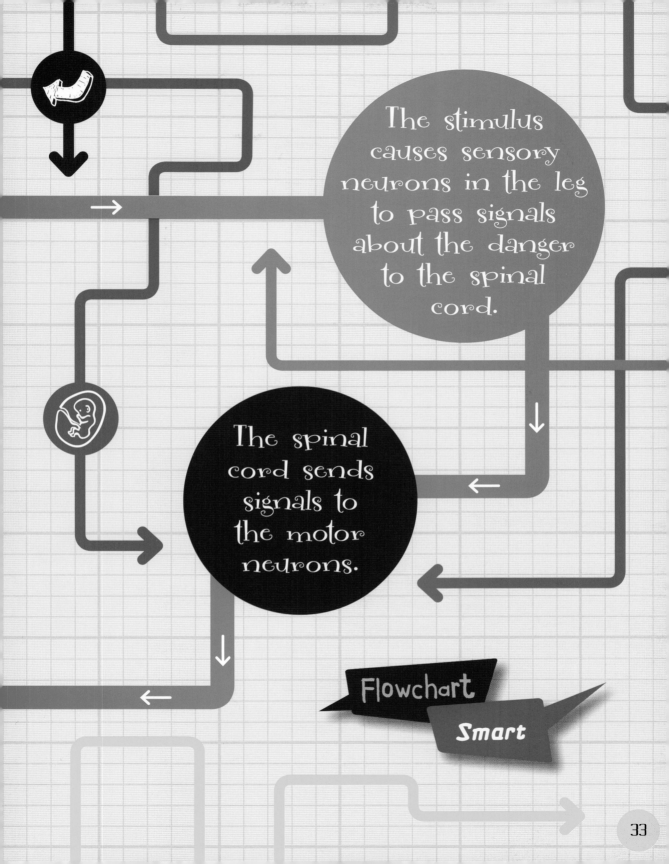

The stimulus causes sensory neurons in the leg to pass signals about the danger to the spinal cord.

The spinal cord sends signals to the motor neurons.

Flowchart Smart

Chapter 5
All in the mind

From the moment we are born, the brain starts to learn about the world. It begins to make memories that shape our response to the world and the people in it.

To learn a new skill, we practise until it becomes easier. By doing something again and again, changes take place in the brain. The neurons that send and receive information about the new skill form new connections and synapses with one another. This creates a new long-term memory about the activity. Once this happens, it is much easier and faster for neurons to signal each other about the new skill.

Long-lasting and structural changes happen in the brain every time people learn. These changes also take place when they have a new thought or memorize new information. Memories are stored in the **hippocampus**. The memory is like the brain's filing system. Using it is a little like storing files in different folders on a computer so that they can be found more easily when needed. When we use our memory, we have to be able to instantly access many different memories at once. For example, when we talk to a friend on the phone, we need to recognize their voice, understand the words they are saying and work out how to answer their questions.

As teachers and parents like to say, "Practice makes perfect". That is because practice creates memories.

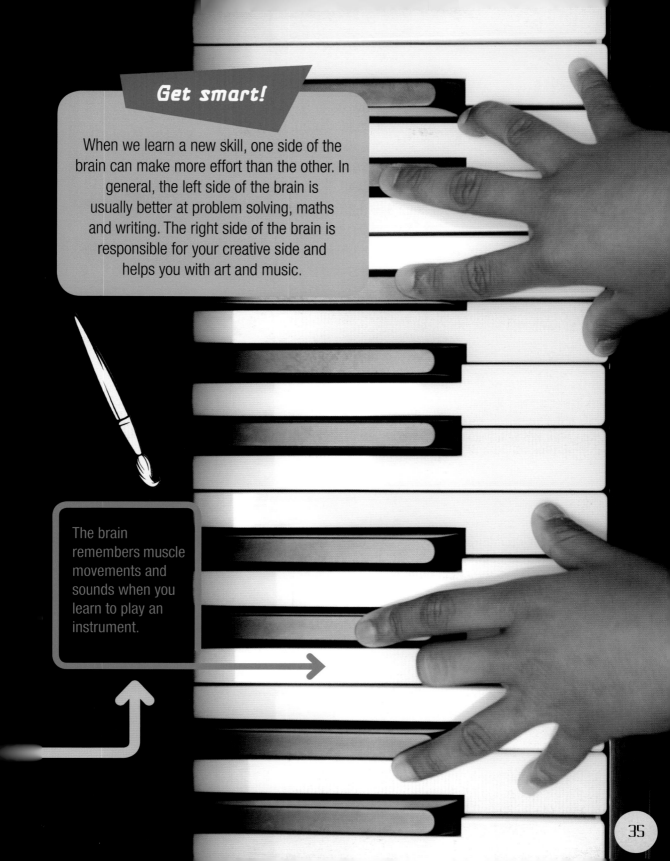

When we learn a new skill, one side of the brain can make more effort than the other. In general, the left side of the brain is usually better at problem solving, maths and writing. The right side of the brain is responsible for your creative side and helps you with art and music.

The brain remembers muscle movements and sounds when you learn to play an instrument.

Emotions

Emotions are important because they allow us to react to situations in appropriate ways. If someone is scared, they try to escape from the danger. If someone is happy, they smile and relax. Long ago, people relied on these emotional reactions to survive. Today, our emotions can still help us.

The limbic system of the brain helps us identify, express and control the body's emotions. The limbic system is located deep inside the brain and includes the hypothalamus, the hippocampus, the **amygdala** and several other nearby areas. When something good happens, the limbic system releases "feel-good" chemicals such as dopamine. Feeling pleasure can make us want to repeat the action that caused it. Eating activates the limbic system, which is very important for our health.

When we are upset, the hypothalamus sends messages to the nervous system, which releases tears from our eyes.

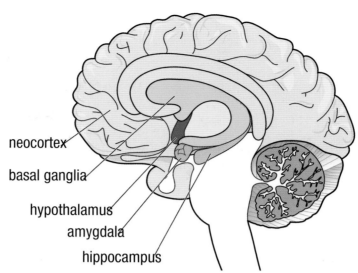

neocortex

basal ganglia

hypothalamus

amygdala

hippocampus

Danger can make people feel angry, frightened or both. These emotions are triggered by the amygdala, which sends signals to the hypothalamus. The hypothalamus is responsible for a lot of the things we do automatically. In this case, it causes immediate changes such as an increase in heart rate and breathing rate. It does this to get the body ready to either attack or run. It helps us react to potentially dangerous situations and stay safe.

The hypothalamus, amygdala and hippocampus are the main areas involved in emotion.

Get smart!

When we remember an event that we found emotional, such as a special birthday party, we recall not only what happened, but also how we felt. This makes it an emotional memory. This type of memory can be triggered by something you heard, saw or smelled at the time, such as birthday candles. Emotional memories can last a very long time.

Get flow chart smart!

Memories

This flow chart follows the stages involved in memory formation.

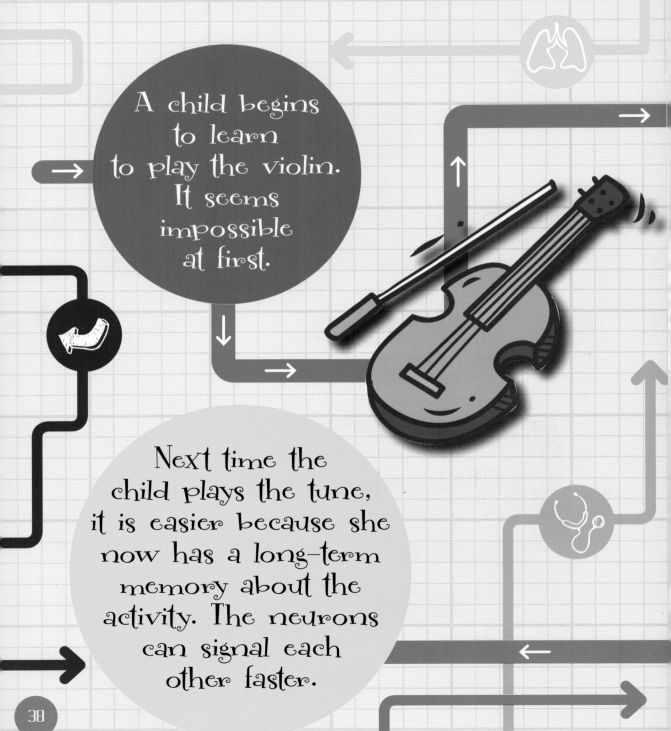

A child begins to learn to play the violin. It seems impossible at first.

Next time the child plays the tune, it is easier because she now has a long-term memory about the activity. The neurons can signal each other faster.

The child practises a tune again and again, making the same movements and hearing the same sounds.

Neurons that send and receive information about these movements and sounds form new connections and synapses with each other.

Flowchart
Smart

Chapter 6
Brain health

The brain is a complex and sensitive organ. To keep the brain healthy, we need a good night's sleep. Sleep gives the brain time to repair itself and build new connections between neurons. We must also eat healthy food and build a healthy pair of lungs so the brain has a steady supply of energy.

Like other cells in the body, neurons combine a type of sugar called glucose with **oxygen** from the air to release the energy they need to do work. The glucose comes from the food we eat. The oxygen comes from air taken into the lungs when we breathe. The oxygen and glucose are regularly delivered to neurons by the blood in blood vessels in the brain.

When we exercise, we breathe faster and deeper, which brings more oxygen into the lungs and the bloodstream. More oxygen is carried in the blood to all parts of the body, including the brain. Exercise also encourages the body to produce a chemical that helps the brain learn for a period of time afterwards. That may be why people who are stuck on a writing or maths problem find it easier to solve after a run around the park.

Eating healthily is important for the brain. In the body, food is broken down and glucose is absorbed into the blood. The brain needs glucose for energy to function.

Taking part in sport is great for your health, but wear a helmet to protect your brain if there's a danger of falling.

Get smart!

The brain is protected by the skull and cushioned by cerebrospinal fluid, but it can still be damaged in a fall or accident. That is why you must wear a helmet when riding a bike or skateboard, and when taking part in any type of sport in which there is a risk of head injury, such as ice hockey or horse riding.

Get flow chart smart!

Brain energy

This flow chart shows how the brain cells obtain the energy they need to work.

When we eat, the body breaks down the food and passes glucose from it into the bloodstream.

The neurons combine glucose with oxygen to release the energy they need to do work.

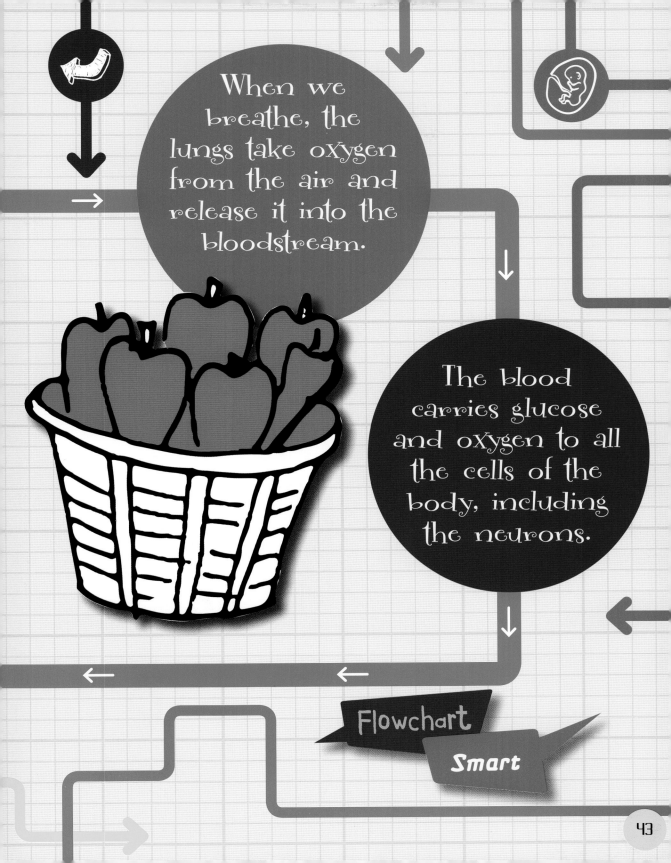

When we breathe, the lungs take oxygen from the air and release it into the bloodstream.

The blood carries glucose and oxygen to all the cells of the body, including the neurons.

Flowchart Smart

Brain games

It is possible to exercise your brain. When you keep your mind as active as possible and make your brain try something new, you can keep it healthy. It becomes more efficient at sorting, storing and retrieving information.

You can improve your memory by playing brain games. These are puzzles that help you learn how to memorize faces, objects and numbers more easily. You can also practise techniques that help you remember lists and facts more quickly. Another way to improve memory and the ability to learn is to read more and to read thoughtfully so you take in all you read. You could also try learning a new word each day, taking up a hobby, joining a new club, learning a language or learning to play an instrument.

The brain and nervous system together form the body's control and communication system. The brain receives and transmits signals from the senses and the rest of the body through neurons. It uses the information it receives to help us learn and feel, and instructs the rest of the body how to respond. The brain helps us in countless ways. Make sure you take care of it!

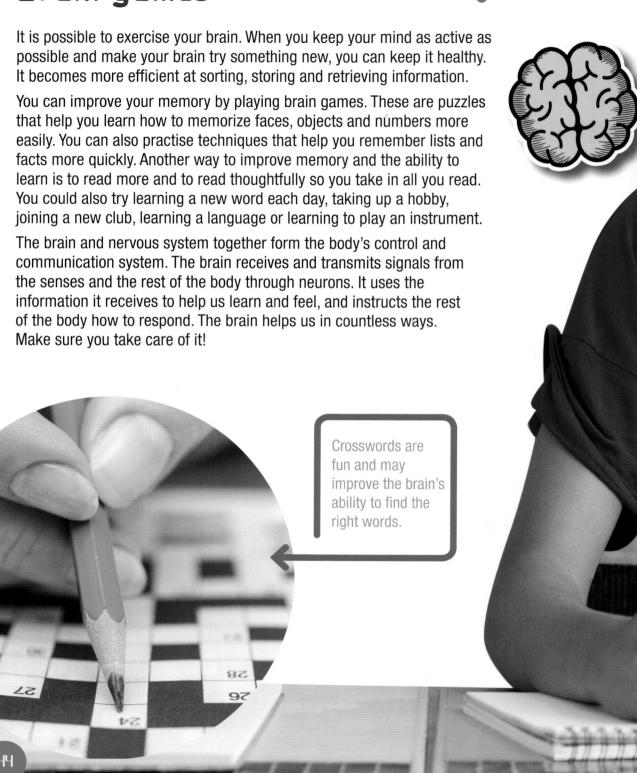

Crosswords are fun and may improve the brain's ability to find the right words.

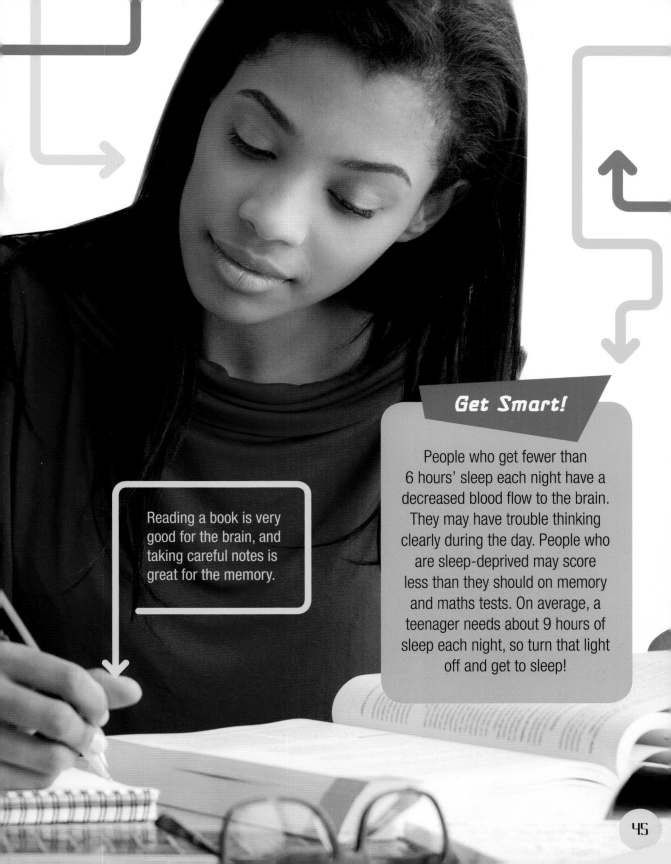

Reading a book is very good for the brain, and taking careful notes is great for the memory.

Get Smart!

People who get fewer than 6 hours' sleep each night have a decreased blood flow to the brain. They may have trouble thinking clearly during the day. People who are sleep-deprived may score less than they should on memory and maths tests. On average, a teenager needs about 9 hours of sleep each night, so turn that light off and get to sleep!

Glossary

amygdala part of the brain that is involved in the processing and expression of emotions

axons long thread-like parts of neurons (nerve cells) along which impulses are conducted from a cell body to other cells

blood vessels tubes that carry blood around the body

brain stem part of the brain that controls the flow of messages between the brain and the rest of the body

cells very small parts that together form all living things

cerebellum part of the brain that controls balance and the use of muscles

cerebrum front part of the brain that is believed to be where thoughts occur

dendrites short branched extensions of a neuron, along which impulses from other cells are transmitted to the cell body

digestive system body parts that together break down food we eat so the body can use it

energy capacity to do work

hippocampus part of the brain involved in making memories, learning and emotions

hormones substances the body makes to influence the way the body grows or develops

hypothalamus area of the brain that helps control glands and body temperature

impulses small amounts of energy that move from one area to another

innate something that people are born with

membranes thin sheets of tissue that usually form a barrier or lining

nerves fibres that carry messages between the brain and the rest of the body

nervous system system of nerves in the body that sends messages between the brain and the other parts of the body

neurons nerve cells

organ body part such as the heart or liver

oxygen gas in the air

pressure pushing force

receptors cells that receive or collect information for the body

spinal cord bundle of nerves inside the spine, which run from the brain down the back

stimuli things or events that start a specific reaction in an organ or tissue

synapse meeting point between two neurons, consisting of a tiny gap across which impulses pass

tissue group of cells of the same type that do a job together, for example muscle cells form muscle tissue

Find out more

Books

Human Body: A Children's Encyclopedia (DK Reference),
DK (DK Children, 2012)

Mental Development: From Birth to Old Age (Your Body for Life), Anna Claybourne (Raintree, 2014)

Understanding Our Head (Brains, Body, Bones!), Lucy Beevor (Raintree, 2017)

Your Brain: Understand it with Numbers (Your Body by Numbers), Melanie Waldron (Raintree, 2014

Websites

Click on the links to play the nervous system game:

www.bbc.co.uk/science/humanbody/body/index_interactivebody.shtml

Find out more about the human brain at:

www.dkfindout.com/uk/human-body/brain-and-nerves/brain/

Index